I Love Ponies...

At the Show

Sandy Ransford

QEB Publishing

Editor: Amanda Askew
Designer: Izzy Langridge

Copyright © QEB Publishing, Inc. 2011

First published in the United States in 2011 by
QEB Publishing. Inc.
3 Wrigley, Suite A
Irvine, CA 92618

www.qed-publishing.co.uk

Library of Congress Cataloging-in-Publication Data

Ransford, Sandy.
 At the show / Sandy Ransford.
    p. cm. -- (I love ponies)
 Includes index.
 Summary: "Covers all the basics of competitive horse riding events for
children, including preparing your horse, getting ready for competition,
and the basics of specific events like show-jumping, dressage, and
more"--Provided by publisher.
 ISBN 978-1-60992-099-9 (library bound)
 1. Horse shows--Juvenile literature. 2. Horsemanship--Juvenile
literature. I. Title. II. Series.

 SF294.7.R36 2012
 636.1--dc22

                       2011009130

ISBN 978 1 60992 099 9

Printed in China

Website information is correct at time of going to press. The publishers
cannot accept liability for the content of the Internet sites that you visit,
nor for any information or links found on third-party websites.

Picture credits
(t=top, b=bottom, l=left, r=right, c=centre, fc=front cover)
All images are courtesy of Bob Langrish images unless stated below.
Alamy 2br Rex Moreton, 9tr PCJones, 9bl The Photolibrary Wales
DK Images 4r John Henderson, 5br Andy Crawford, 6r Bob Langrish,
7br Andy Crawford, 15b Dorling Kindersley,
Dreamstime 2mr Harperdrewart,
Shutterstock 3br Groomee, nito

Words in **bold** are explained in the Glossary on page 22.

Remember!
Children must always wear appropriate clothing, including a riding hat, and follow safety guidelines when handling or riding horses and ponies.

Contents

Preparing your Pony

When you enter your pony in a competition, it must look its best—clean and well groomed—to help you and your pony do the best you can.

You can trim the long hair on a pony's **fetlocks** and mane. To trim the tail, ask someone to hold it out slightly, so you can trim it neatly and level.

Grooming
To get your pony's coat gleaming, you need to groom it well with a **body brush**. Then give it a final polish with a cotton cloth to remove dust and loose hairs.

Quarter Marks
Patterns made on the pony's quarters using a comb, or a stencil and a damp water brush, are called quarter marks. Brush or comb the hair in different directions to create the effect.

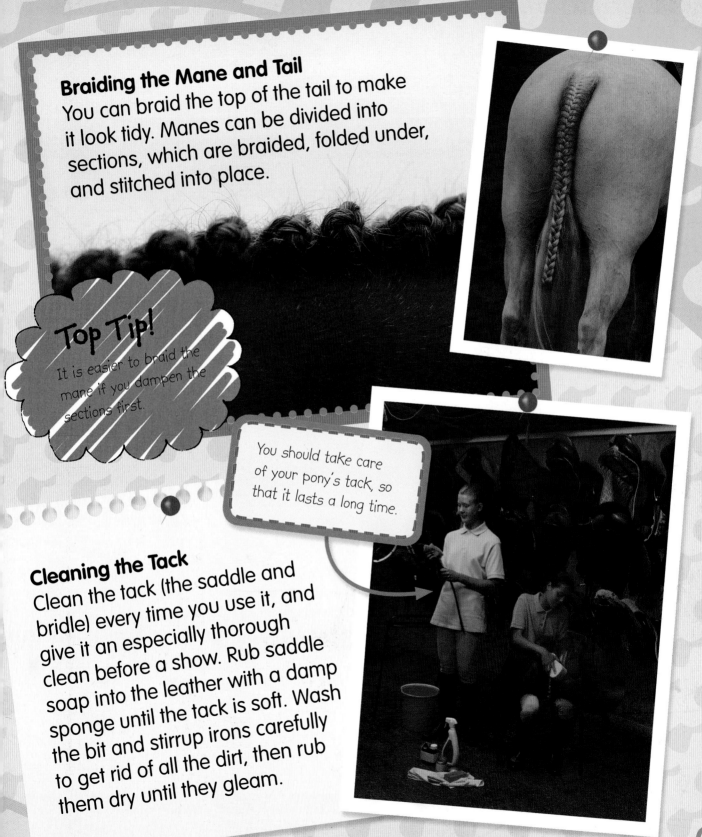

Braiding the Mane and Tail

You can braid the top of the tail to make it look tidy. Manes can be divided into sections, which are braided, folded under, and stitched into place.

Top Tip!

It is easier to braid the mane if you dampen the sections first.

You should take care of your pony's tack, so that it lasts a long time.

Cleaning the Tack

Clean the tack (the saddle and bridle) every time you use it, and give it an especially thorough clean before a show. Rub saddle soap into the leather with a damp sponge until the tack is soft. Wash the bit and stirrup irons carefully to get rid of all the dirt, then rub them dry until they gleam.

At the Show

If you are going to ride in a show, make sure that you look as neat and clean as your pony. When you're at a show, rest your pony between classes. Let it graze, and give it a drink of water.

riding hat

shirt and tie

gloves

riding jacket

jodhpurs

riding boots

Riding Clothing
At a show, you need to wear proper riding clothes— jodhpurs with riding boots, a shirt and tie, a riding coat, gloves, and your riding hat. Your clothes should be clean and tidy, and your boots must be well polished.

At many shows, you will be required to wear a safety vest. This protects your back from injury should you fall off.

Arriving

Try to arrive at a show with plenty of time to spare. Register for your class then, while you are waiting to be called, make sure your pony is clean, tidy, and comfortable.

If you're in a jumping class, you will be able to jump over a few practice rails while you wait.

In the Collecting Ring

The collecting ring is a small ring near the entrance to the main ring, where competitors wait until it is time for their class. You may want to practice your trot and canter, but don't work the pony too hard. You don't want it to be sweating when you enter the ring.

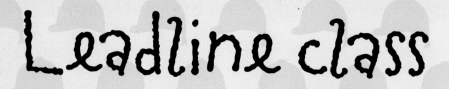

Leadline class

If you are young and new to riding, your first **showing** class may well be on a leadline. A parent or other adult will lead the pony around while you ride as well as you can.

Correct Dress

In a leadline class the handler, as well as the rider, has to wear the right clothes. For men, this is a suit, a tie, gloves, and a hat; for women, this is a skirt, coat, hat, and gloves.

This pony, its rider, and handler all look very elegant.

In the Ring

The leadline competitors walk, then trot, around the ring together. The judge then calls them in to line up, and each does an **individual show**, such as trotting a circle in each direction.

The handler needs to be able to run when leading the pony.

Choosing the Winner

When everyone has done their show, the ponies walk round again. Then, they line up in winning order—first, second, third, and so on. The first four or five receive a ribbon.

First Riding and Showing Classes

Many shows have a special class for young riders who are competing in a show for the first time off the leadline.

First Ridden Classes

These classes are for young riders, but this time you ride alone. The ponies go around together in both walk and trot, and then line up—as in the leadline class. The judge examines the ponies one at a time, and you each do an individual show. In this class you may canter, as well as walk and trot, in your show.

walk

trot

canter

Categories of Showing Class

Height	Rider Age
Up to 12. 2 hh (50 inches or 128 cm)	Up to 13 years
12. 2 hh to 13.2 hh (54 inches or 138 cm)	Up to 15 years
13.2 hh to 14.2 hh (59 inches or 148 cm)	Up to 17 years

The height of a horse or pony is measured in hands. One hand is equal to 4 inches (10.16 centimeters).

Showing Classes

Similar to the first riding classes, the showing classes allow you to canter around the ring together, as well as walk and trot. You will also have to dismount, remove your pony's saddle, and walk and trot it out to show the judge how well your pony moves.

Winning a Ribbon

If you win a ribbon, the judge fixes it to the pony's bridle, or to the string of your number. You will canter around the ring in a lap of honor, in the order of judging. When the spectators clap, be sure you have control of your pony, or it may get over excited.

Leading an unridden horse or pony around a show ring is called showing **in hand**.

Show Jumping

These classes combine the skills needed for both showing classes and show jumping.

In the Ring

A working hunter pony is expected to do all the things a show pony does, as well as gallop and jump. In Phase One, each competitor goes around the jumping course in turn. In Phase Two, the whole class goes around the ring together in walk, trot, and canter. Finally, the ponies gallop around the ring one at a time.

It's Showtime!
A score is given for each phase. The scores are added together to find the winner.

The course might include jumps such as these rails. They won't be too high.

Show Jumping

This sport involves riding around a course and going over many different types of jump. The jumps are colored and have different distances between them.

Preparing to Jump

You can walk around a show jumping course before the class and work out how many strides you need to take when approaching each jump. The jumps are numbered to help you find your way. Competitors jump the course one at a time.

The Scoring System

Each competitor collects **faults** for knocking down jumps, refusing to go over them, missing one, or going over the time limit. The rider with the smallest number of faults wins.

Types of Jump

Show jumping rings contain "spread" jumps such as an oxer, and "uprights" such as a wall. The "bricks" are wooden blocks that are easy to knock down without injuring the pony.

Oxer

Crossed Rails

Wall

Pony Show Games

Entering games classes is a lot of fun. Many of the games are races, and you need a speedy pony that will turn and stop when and where you want it to. It is useful to be able to vault on to your pony to save time.

With plenty of practice, you can vault on to a pony while it's moving.

Bending Race
This race needs a well trained pony. You have to bend your way along a line of upright poles, turn at the end, then bend your way back again.

Potato Race

In this race, you have to pick up a potato, gallop down the field, and then put it in a pail. You then go back for the next potato, and the person who gets all their potatoes in the pail first is the winner.

Ball and Spoon Race

Carrying a ball on a spoon while running as fast as you can or leading your pony is not easy. If you drop your ball, you have to stop and pick it up again.

Sack Race

In this race, you canter down the field, get off your pony, and climb into a sack. Then, leading your pony, you get back to the start as fast as you can. Most people jump along, holding the pony with one hand, and the sack with the other.

Handy Pony Class

For the handy pony, or handy ranch, class you need an obedient, calm, well-behaved pony. In this class, you have to do all types of unusual tasks while riding your pony.

A task may involve walking or trotting over a number of rails laid on the ground.

You may have to lead your pony while balancing along a line of upturned pots.

There will be tasks where you need to dismount, pick something up, then mount again and take the object to another part of the ring.

It's Showtime!
Your pony should learn how to stand still while you lean over and move around in the saddle.

These riders are rearranging jumbled up letters so they spell out the words "PONY CLUB."

These classes are great fun to watch.

Dress Up Class

This is a lot of fun! At dress up class you and your pony wear a costume. You are a character, so you need to plan your outfit, and your pony's. You may need some help making it. The best costume wins.

Spots Before your Eyes
This rider has made her pony match her costume by painting spots on it. If you do this, use only water based paint so you can wash it off again.

This young rider has used pink paint on the pony's mane and tail, and given it a paper horn to look like a unicorn!

Western Dress

Clothing worn for Western riding events—such as reining, cutting, and rodeo—consists of jeans, cowboy boots, a cowboy hat, a long sleeved shirt, and protective leather leggings called chaps. Bright colors and fancy patterns are popular.

At Christmas, you could wear a Santa or elf costume. Then turn your pony into Rudolph the Red Nosed Reindeer.

Christmas Cheer

Fix fake antlers to your pony's bridle and paint its nose red with water based paint. Then twist a tinsel garland around the bridle, draping it over the pony's neck.

Dressage and Eventing

Dressage and eventing are competitions for experienced riders. In dressage, your pony has to perform precise movements and paces.

The Dressage Arena
A dressage arena has a low fence around it and letters along the sides. Most arenas measure 130 feet (40 meters) by 65 feet (20 meters), but for some international competitions, they are 195 feet (60 meters) by 65 feet (20 meters).

Markers around an arena 130 by 65 feet or 40 by 20 meters

A

F

D

K

B

X

E

M

G

H

C

You have to learn the test first—although in some **novice** tests, it may be read out to you. For example, you might walk into the arena at A, trot to C, canter from C to F, walk from F to E, and so on.

Advanced tasks include changes of leg at every stride in canter, pirouettes, and piaffe—a kind of slow trotting on the spot.

Eventing

This sport involves dressage, cross country, and show jumping. In the cross country section, you ride a course of difficult jumps within a set time. The course usually involves jumping into and out of a lake.

Cross Country

To ride "cross-country" means galloping over a course of jumps set out in fields and wooded areas. You have to be an experienced rider, with a bold, brave horse or pony.

Hunter Trials

These are jumping competitions ridden across fields and through woods, for both horses and ponies. You may also have to open and close gates. There is usually a set time in which the course has to be completed.

Glossary

Body brush A short-bristled brush used for removing dirt and grease from a pony's coat.

Dressage A competition in which a horse or pony has to carry out precise movements and paces.

Faults Penalty points collected in jumping competitions.

Fetlocks The lowest joints in a horse or pony's legs, just above the hooves.

Individual show A display of your pony's movement and paces, carried out in a showing class.

In hand Leading an unridden horse or pony while on foot.

Novice A pony or rider that is inexperienced in what it is doing.

Showing Exhibiting a horse or pony at a show, where it is judged on its obedience, paces, and behavior.

Index

Notes for Parents and Teachers

All shows, games, and competitions have sets of rules that have to be adhered to. If you are new to competing, you should familiarize yourself with them before entering young riders. Make sure the rider is wearing the correct form of clothing, and that they understand what entering the class involves.

Whatever kind of class the child enters, make sure they practice with the pony as much as possible, so, by the time of the competition, they both know exactly what they are doing. It's best to keep an individual show simple, but to carry out each pace and change of pace as well as possible. Teach the pony to do a good, square halt, with both forefeet and both hind feet in line with each other, and make sure the pony will stand until told to move on again.

Encourage the child to watch other classes, to see how the ponies perform and how well the riders ride them. If a pony is particularly well schooled, see if the child can work out exactly what the rider does to get it to move so well.

When watching jumping classes, point out how many strides different ponies take on approaching a jump. Ask the child to imagine how many strides they would need to take on their pony.

It's fun to construct miniature show jumps at home. Pencils can be painted to make rails, matchboxes to make walls, and small twigs between two pencils tied together with string will make a brush fence. Even if children ride ponies, they will enjoy playing with toy ponies and jumps on a rainy day.

Horse and pony websites

www.ponyclub.org
The Pony Club

www.aqha.com
American Quarter Horse Association

www.usef.org
United States Equestrian Federation

www.horsesport.org
Fédération Equestre Internationale (the international body that regulates equestrian sport)

www.worldhorsewelfare.org
World Horse Welfare